50 Comfort Home Canadian Dishes

By: Kelly Johnson

Table of Contents

- Classic Poutine
- Tourtière (French Canadian Meat Pie)
- Butter Tarts
- Maple-Glazed Salmon
- Nanaimo Bars
- Split Pea Soup with Ham
- Bison Meatloaf
- Wild Rice and Mushroom Soup
- Roasted Root Vegetables
- Prairie Wheat Pancakes
- Saskatoon Berry Pie
- Creamy Potato and Leek Soup
- Maple Baked Beans
- Homemade Bannock
- Cranberry-Maple Turkey Meatballs
- Cheddar and Chive Biscuits
- Roasted Pumpkin Soup
- Farmhouse Mac and Cheese
- Wild Blueberry Muffins
- Tourtière Hand Pies
- Canadian Cheddar Soup
- Maple-Glazed Pork Chops
- Apple and Cinnamon Crisp
- Honey-Glazed Carrots and Parsnips
- Creamy Corn Chowder
- Roasted Garlic Mashed Potatoes
- Sweet Corn Fritters
- Grilled Arctic Char with Dill Butter
- Traditional Prairie Perogies
- Barley and Beef Stew
- Classic Montreal Smoked Meat Sandwich
- Roasted Brussels Sprouts with Bacon
- Chokecherry Syrup Pancakes
- Wheat Berry and Cranberry Salad
- Oatmeal Maple Cookies

- Maple Butter Glazed Chicken
- Homemade Rhubarb Crisp
- Barbecue Bison Ribs
- Farmer's Market Vegetable Stir-Fry
- Traditional Tourtière with Ketchup Chutney
- Smoked Trout with Horseradish Cream
- Apple and Cheddar Hand Pies
- Wild Rice and Lentil Pilaf
- Cranberry Scones
- Maple-Glazed Roast Chicken
- Venison Chili
- Roasted Chestnut and Mushroom Soup
- Rye Bread with Flax Seeds
- Pumpkin Seed and Cranberry Energy Bites
- Maple-Glazed Donuts

Classic Poutine

Ingredients:

- 4 large russet potatoes, cut into fries
- Oil for frying
- 1 cup cheese curds
- 2 cups beef or mushroom gravy

Instructions:

1. Heat oil in a fryer to 375°F (190°C). Fry potatoes until golden and crispy. Drain on paper towels.
2. Place fries on a serving plate, top with cheese curds, and pour hot gravy over.
3. Serve immediately.

Tourtière (French Canadian Meat Pie)

Ingredients:

- 1 lb ground pork
- 1/2 lb ground beef
- 1 small onion, finely chopped
- 2 cloves garlic, minced
- 1/2 tsp ground cinnamon
- 1/4 tsp ground cloves
- 1/2 tsp dried thyme
- 1/2 tsp salt
- 1/4 tsp black pepper
- 1/2 cup beef broth
- 1/2 cup mashed potatoes
- 1 double-crust pie dough

Instructions:

1. Preheat oven to 375°F (190°C).
2. In a pan, cook pork and beef over medium heat until browned. Drain excess fat.
3. Add onion, garlic, cinnamon, cloves, thyme, salt, and pepper. Cook until onions are soft.
4. Stir in broth and mashed potatoes. Let cool.
5. Roll out pie dough and place in a pie dish. Fill with meat mixture and cover with the second crust.
6. Crimp edges and cut slits in the top. Bake for 35-40 minutes until golden. Cool before serving.

Butter Tarts

Ingredients:

Pastry:

- 1 1/4 cups all-purpose flour
- 1/2 cup cold butter, cubed
- 1/4 tsp salt
- 3 tbsp cold water

Filling:

- 1/2 cup brown sugar
- 1/2 cup pure maple syrup
- 1/4 cup melted butter
- 1 egg, beaten
- 1 tsp vanilla extract
- 1/2 cup raisins or chopped pecans

Instructions:

1. Preheat oven to 375°F (190°C).
2. For pastry, mix flour and salt. Cut in butter until crumbly. Add water and mix until dough forms. Chill for 30 minutes.
3. Roll out dough and cut into rounds. Place in tart tins.
4. Whisk filling ingredients and pour into shells.
5. Bake for 20-25 minutes until filling is set. Cool before serving.

Maple-Glazed Salmon

Ingredients:

- 2 salmon fillets
- 1/4 cup pure maple syrup
- 1 tbsp Dijon mustard
- 1 tbsp soy sauce
- 1 tsp lemon juice
- 1/2 tsp black pepper

Instructions:

1. Preheat oven to 400°F (200°C).
2. In a small bowl, mix maple syrup, mustard, soy sauce, lemon juice, and pepper.
3. Place salmon on a baking sheet and brush with glaze.
4. Bake for 12-15 minutes until flaky. Serve warm.

Nanaimo Bars

Ingredients:

Base:

- 1/2 cup butter, melted
- 1/4 cup sugar
- 1/3 cup cocoa powder
- 1 egg, beaten
- 1 tsp vanilla extract
- 2 cups graham cracker crumbs
- 1 cup shredded coconut

Filling:

- 1/2 cup butter, softened
- 2 cups powdered sugar
- 2 tbsp custard powder
- 3 tbsp milk

Topping:

- 4 oz semi-sweet chocolate, melted
- 2 tbsp butter

Instructions:

1. Mix base ingredients and press into a greased pan. Chill for 15 minutes.
2. Beat filling ingredients until smooth, spread over base, and chill for another 15 minutes.
3. Melt chocolate with butter and spread over the filling. Chill until set, then cut into squares.

Split Pea Soup with Ham

Ingredients:

- 1 cup dried split peas, rinsed
- 1 small onion, chopped
- 1 carrot, diced
- 2 cloves garlic, minced
- 4 cups chicken broth
- 1 cup diced ham
- 1 bay leaf
- 1/2 tsp dried thyme
- Salt and pepper to taste

Instructions:

1. In a pot, sauté onion, carrot, and garlic until softened.
2. Add peas, broth, ham, bay leaf, thyme, salt, and pepper.
3. Bring to a boil, then reduce heat and simmer for 45-50 minutes until peas are soft.
4. Remove bay leaf and serve warm.

Bison Meatloaf

Ingredients:

- 1 lb ground bison
- 1/2 cup cooked wild rice
- 1 small onion, chopped
- 1 egg
- 1/4 cup breadcrumbs
- 2 tbsp ketchup
- 1 tbsp Worcestershire sauce
- 1/2 tsp salt
- 1/4 tsp black pepper

Instructions:

1. Preheat oven to 375°F (190°C).
2. In a bowl, mix all ingredients until well combined.
3. Shape into a loaf and place in a greased pan.
4. Bake for 45-50 minutes until cooked through. Let rest before slicing.

Wild Rice and Mushroom Soup

Ingredients:

- 1/2 cup wild rice
- 4 cups vegetable broth
- 1 tbsp butter
- 1 small onion, chopped
- 2 cloves garlic, minced
- 1 cup mushrooms, sliced
- 1/2 tsp dried thyme
- 1/2 cup heavy cream
- Salt and pepper to taste

Instructions:

1. In a saucepan, cook wild rice in vegetable broth for 40 minutes until tender.
2. In a pot, melt butter and sauté onion, garlic, and mushrooms.
3. Add cooked wild rice and remaining broth. Simmer for 10 minutes.
4. Stir in heavy cream, thyme, salt, and pepper. Serve warm.

Roasted Root Vegetables

Ingredients:

- 2 carrots, sliced
- 2 parsnips, sliced
- 1 sweet potato, cubed
- 1 tbsp olive oil
- 1 tsp dried rosemary
- Salt and pepper to taste

Instructions:

1. Preheat oven to 400°F (200°C).
2. Toss vegetables with oil, rosemary, salt, and pepper.
3. Roast for 35-40 minutes, stirring occasionally. Serve warm.

Prairie Wheat Pancakes

Ingredients:

- 1 cup whole wheat flour
- 1/2 cup all-purpose flour
- 1 tbsp baking powder
- 1/2 tsp salt
- 1 1/4 cups milk
- 1 egg
- 2 tbsp maple syrup
- 2 tbsp melted butter

Instructions:

1. In a bowl, whisk flours, baking powder, and salt.
2. In another bowl, mix milk, egg, maple syrup, and melted butter.
3. Combine wet and dry ingredients.
4. Cook pancakes on a hot griddle until golden brown.

Saskatoon Berry Pie

Ingredients:

- 2 1/2 cups Saskatoon berries
- 3/4 cup sugar
- 1 tbsp lemon juice
- 1/4 cup water
- 2 tbsp cornstarch
- 1/2 tsp cinnamon
- 1 prepared pie crust

Instructions:

1. Preheat oven to 375°F (190°C).
2. In a saucepan, combine berries, sugar, lemon juice, and water. Simmer for 5 minutes.
3. Stir in cornstarch and cinnamon. Cook until thickened.
4. Pour filling into pie crust. Cover with top crust or lattice.
5. Bake for 40-45 minutes until golden brown. Cool before serving.

Creamy Potato and Leek Soup

Ingredients:

- 3 large potatoes, peeled and diced
- 2 leeks, sliced
- 3 cups vegetable broth
- 1/2 cup heavy cream
- 2 tbsp butter
- 2 cloves garlic, minced
- Salt and pepper to taste

Instructions:

1. In a pot, melt butter and sauté leeks and garlic until soft.
2. Add potatoes and broth. Simmer for 20 minutes until potatoes are tender.
3. Blend until smooth, then stir in heavy cream. Season to taste and serve warm.

Maple Baked Beans

Ingredients:

- 2 cups dried navy beans
- 4 cups water
- 1/2 cup pure maple syrup
- 1/2 cup ketchup
- 1 tbsp Dijon mustard
- 1 small onion, diced
- 4 slices bacon, chopped
- 1 tsp salt
- 1/2 tsp black pepper

Instructions:

1. Soak beans overnight. Drain and rinse.
2. In a pot, bring beans and water to a boil. Simmer for 1 hour.
3. Preheat oven to 300°F (150°C).
4. In a baking dish, mix beans with maple syrup, ketchup, mustard, onion, bacon, salt, and pepper.
5. Cover and bake for 3-4 hours, stirring occasionally. Serve warm.

Homemade Bannock

Ingredients:

- 2 cups all-purpose flour
- 1 tbsp baking powder
- 1/2 tsp salt
- 1/4 cup butter, melted
- 3/4 cup water

Instructions:

1. Preheat oven to 375°F (190°C).
2. In a bowl, mix flour, baking powder, and salt.
3. Stir in melted butter and water until a dough forms.
4. Shape into a round and place on a greased baking sheet.
5. Bake for 25-30 minutes until golden brown. Serve warm.

Cranberry-Maple Turkey Meatballs

Ingredients:

- 1 lb ground turkey
- 1/4 cup breadcrumbs
- 1/4 cup dried cranberries, chopped
- 1 egg
- 1 tbsp maple syrup
- 1/2 tsp dried sage
- 1/2 tsp salt
- 1/4 tsp black pepper
- 1 tbsp olive oil

Instructions:

1. Preheat oven to 375°F (190°C).
2. In a bowl, mix turkey, breadcrumbs, cranberries, egg, maple syrup, sage, salt, and pepper.
3. Shape into small meatballs.
4. Heat olive oil in a skillet and brown meatballs on all sides.
5. Transfer to a baking dish and bake for 15 minutes until cooked through. Serve warm.

Cheddar and Chive Biscuits

Ingredients:

- 2 cups all-purpose flour
- 1 tbsp baking powder
- 1/2 tsp salt
- 1/2 cup cold butter, cubed
- 1 cup shredded cheddar cheese
- 1/4 cup chopped chives
- 3/4 cup milk

Instructions:

1. Preheat oven to 375°F (190°C).
2. In a bowl, mix flour, baking powder, and salt.
3. Cut in butter until mixture is crumbly. Stir in cheese and chives.
4. Add milk and mix until dough forms.
5. Drop spoonfuls onto a baking sheet and bake for 15-18 minutes.

Roasted Pumpkin Soup

Ingredients:

- 4 cups pumpkin, cubed
- 1 small onion, chopped
- 2 cloves garlic, minced
- 3 cups vegetable broth
- 1/2 cup coconut milk
- 1 tsp ground cumin
- 1/2 tsp cinnamon
- Salt and pepper to taste
- 1 tbsp olive oil

Instructions:

1. Preheat oven to 400°F (200°C). Toss pumpkin with olive oil and roast for 25-30 minutes.
2. In a pot, sauté onion and garlic until soft. Add roasted pumpkin.
3. Pour in broth and bring to a simmer. Blend until smooth.
4. Stir in coconut milk, cumin, cinnamon, salt, and pepper. Simmer for 5 more minutes. Serve warm.

Farmhouse Mac and Cheese

Ingredients:

- 2 cups elbow macaroni
- 2 tbsp butter
- 2 tbsp flour
- 2 cups milk
- 2 cups sharp cheddar cheese, shredded
- 1/2 tsp mustard powder
- 1/2 tsp salt
- 1/4 tsp black pepper

Instructions:

1. Cook macaroni according to package instructions. Drain and set aside.
2. In a saucepan, melt butter and whisk in flour to form a roux.
3. Gradually whisk in milk and cook until thickened.
4. Stir in cheese, mustard powder, salt, and pepper.
5. Mix sauce with macaroni and serve warm.

Wild Blueberry Muffins

Ingredients:

- 2 cups all-purpose flour
- 1/2 cup sugar
- 1 tbsp baking powder
- 1/2 tsp salt
- 1 cup wild blueberries
- 1 cup milk
- 1/3 cup butter, melted
- 1 egg
- 1 tsp vanilla extract

Instructions:

1. Preheat oven to 375°F (190°C).
2. In a bowl, mix flour, sugar, baking powder, and salt.
3. In another bowl, whisk milk, butter, egg, and vanilla.
4. Combine wet and dry ingredients, then fold in blueberries.
5. Spoon batter into a muffin tin and bake for 18-20 minutes.

Tourtière Hand Pies

Ingredients:

- 1/2 lb ground pork
- 1/2 lb ground beef
- 1 small onion, finely chopped
- 1 clove garlic, minced
- 1/2 tsp ground cinnamon
- 1/4 tsp ground cloves
- 1/2 tsp salt
- 1/4 tsp black pepper
- 1/2 cup beef broth
- 1 sheet puff pastry, thawed
- 1 egg, beaten

Instructions:

1. Preheat oven to 375°F (190°C).
2. Cook pork and beef in a pan over medium heat until browned. Drain fat.
3. Add onion, garlic, cinnamon, cloves, salt, and pepper. Cook until onions soften.
4. Stir in broth and simmer for 5 minutes. Let cool.
5. Roll out puff pastry and cut into squares. Fill with meat mixture, fold over, and seal edges.
6. Brush with egg wash and bake for 20-25 minutes until golden brown.

Canadian Cheddar Soup

Ingredients:

- 2 tbsp butter
- 1 small onion, diced
- 2 cloves garlic, minced
- 2 tbsp flour
- 3 cups chicken broth
- 1 cup heavy cream
- 2 cups sharp cheddar cheese, shredded
- 1/2 tsp mustard powder
- Salt and pepper to taste

Instructions:

1. Melt butter in a pot over medium heat. Sauté onion and garlic until soft.
2. Stir in flour and cook for 1 minute.
3. Add broth and simmer for 5 minutes. Stir in cream and cheese.
4. Season with mustard powder, salt, and pepper. Serve warm.

Maple-Glazed Pork Chops

Ingredients:

- 2 pork chops
- 1/4 cup pure maple syrup
- 1 tbsp Dijon mustard
- 1 tbsp soy sauce
- 1/2 tsp black pepper

Instructions:

1. Preheat oven to 375°F (190°C).
2. Mix maple syrup, mustard, soy sauce, and pepper.
3. Brush glaze on pork chops and bake for 20-25 minutes, basting halfway through.
4. Serve warm.

Apple and Cinnamon Crisp

Ingredients:

Filling:

- 4 cups apples, peeled and sliced
- 1/4 cup sugar
- 1 tbsp lemon juice
- 1/2 tsp cinnamon

Topping:

- 1 cup rolled oats
- 1/2 cup flour
- 1/3 cup brown sugar
- 1/2 tsp cinnamon
- 1/2 cup butter, melted

Instructions:

1. Preheat oven to 375°F (190°C).
2. Toss apples with sugar, lemon juice, and cinnamon. Spread in a baking dish.
3. Mix oats, flour, brown sugar, cinnamon, and melted butter. Sprinkle over apples.
4. Bake for 35-40 minutes until golden and bubbly. Serve warm.

Honey-Glazed Carrots and Parsnips

Ingredients:

- 2 carrots, sliced
- 2 parsnips, sliced
- 1 tbsp butter
- 1 tbsp honey
- 1/2 tsp salt

Instructions:

1. Sauté carrots and parsnips in butter for 5 minutes.
2. Drizzle with honey and salt. Cook until tender. Serve warm.

Creamy Corn Chowder

Ingredients:

- 2 tbsp butter
- 1 small onion, diced
- 2 cloves garlic, minced
- 2 medium potatoes, diced
- 3 cups corn kernels (fresh or frozen)
- 3 cups vegetable or chicken broth
- 1 cup heavy cream
- 1/2 tsp dried thyme
- Salt and pepper to taste
- 2 tbsp chopped fresh parsley

Instructions:

1. In a pot, melt butter over medium heat. Sauté onion and garlic until soft.
2. Add potatoes, corn, broth, thyme, salt, and pepper. Simmer for 15 minutes until potatoes are tender.
3. Stir in heavy cream and cook for 5 more minutes.
4. Garnish with parsley and serve warm.

Roasted Garlic Mashed Potatoes

Ingredients:

- 4 large potatoes, peeled and diced
- 1 head garlic, roasted
- 1/2 cup heavy cream
- 2 tbsp butter
- Salt and pepper to taste

Instructions:

1. Boil potatoes until fork-tender, then drain.
2. Squeeze roasted garlic cloves into the potatoes.
3. Mash with butter, cream, salt, and pepper until smooth. Serve warm.

Sweet Corn Fritters

Ingredients:

- 1 cup fresh or frozen corn kernels
- 1/2 cup all-purpose flour
- 1/4 cup cornmeal
- 1/2 tsp baking powder
- 1/2 tsp salt
- 1/4 tsp black pepper
- 1/4 cup milk
- 1 egg
- 1 tbsp chopped green onions
- 1 tbsp butter or oil for frying

Instructions:

1. In a bowl, mix flour, cornmeal, baking powder, salt, and pepper.
2. Stir in milk, egg, and green onions. Fold in corn.
3. Heat butter in a skillet over medium heat. Drop spoonfuls of batter and cook for 2-3 minutes per side until golden.
4. Serve warm.

Grilled Arctic Char with Dill Butter

Ingredients:

- 2 Arctic char fillets
- 2 tbsp butter, melted
- 1 tbsp fresh dill, chopped
- 1 tsp lemon zest
- Salt and pepper to taste
- Lemon wedges for serving

Instructions:

1. Preheat grill to medium heat.
2. Mix butter, dill, lemon zest, salt, and pepper.
3. Brush fillets with mixture and grill for 4-5 minutes per side.
4. Serve with lemon wedges.

Traditional Prairie Perogies

Ingredients:

Dough:

- 2 cups all-purpose flour
- 1/2 tsp salt
- 1/2 cup sour cream
- 1 egg
- 1/4 cup water

Filling:

- 1 cup mashed potatoes
- 1/2 cup cheddar cheese, shredded
- 1/4 tsp salt
- 1/4 tsp black pepper

Instructions:

1. Mix dough ingredients in a bowl, knead until smooth, and let rest for 30 minutes.
2. In a bowl, mix mashed potatoes, cheddar cheese, salt, and pepper.
3. Roll out dough and cut into circles. Place filling in the center of each circle.
4. Fold over and pinch edges to seal.
5. Boil perogies in salted water until they float. Drain and serve with butter or sour cream.

Barley and Beef Stew

Ingredients:

- 1 lb beef stew meat, cubed
- 1 tbsp oil
- 1 onion, chopped
- 2 carrots, diced
- 2 celery stalks, chopped
- 3 cloves garlic, minced
- 1/2 cup pearl barley
- 4 cups beef broth
- 1 tsp dried thyme
- 1 bay leaf
- Salt and pepper to taste

Instructions:

1. Heat oil in a pot and brown beef. Remove and set aside.
2. Sauté onion, carrots, celery, and garlic until soft.
3. Add barley, beef, broth, thyme, bay leaf, salt, and pepper.
4. Simmer for 1.5 hours until beef is tender. Remove bay leaf before serving.

Classic Montreal Smoked Meat Sandwich

Ingredients:

- 1/2 lb Montreal smoked meat, sliced
- 2 slices rye bread
- 1 tbsp yellow mustard

Instructions:

1. Warm smoked meat by steaming for a few minutes.
2. Spread mustard on one slice of rye bread.
3. Pile smoked meat onto the bread and top with the other slice.
4. Serve warm with pickles on the side.

Roasted Brussels Sprouts with Bacon

Ingredients:

- 1 lb Brussels sprouts, halved
- 4 slices bacon, chopped
- 2 tbsp olive oil
- 1 tbsp balsamic vinegar
- Salt and pepper to taste

Instructions:

1. Preheat oven to 400°F (200°C).
2. Toss Brussels sprouts with olive oil, salt, and pepper.
3. Spread on a baking sheet and sprinkle with bacon.
4. Roast for 20-25 minutes, stirring occasionally.
5. Drizzle with balsamic vinegar before serving.

Chokecherry Syrup Pancakes

Ingredients:

Pancakes:

- 1 cup all-purpose flour
- 1 tbsp sugar
- 1 tsp baking powder
- 1/2 tsp baking soda
- 1/4 tsp salt
- 1 cup buttermilk
- 1 egg
- 1 tbsp melted butter

Chokecherry Syrup:

- 2 cups chokecherries
- 1 cup water
- 1 cup sugar

Instructions:

1. For syrup, simmer chokecherries and water for 15 minutes. Strain and return liquid to pot.
2. Add sugar and simmer until thickened.
3. For pancakes, mix dry ingredients. Whisk wet ingredients separately and combine.
4. Cook pancakes on a hot griddle until golden.
5. Serve with chokecherry syrup.

Wheat Berry and Cranberry Salad

Ingredients:

- 1 cup cooked wheat berries
- 1/2 cup dried cranberries
- 1/4 cup chopped pecans
- 1/4 cup diced celery
- 1/4 cup crumbled feta
- 2 tbsp olive oil
- 1 tbsp balsamic vinegar
- Salt and pepper to taste

Instructions:

1. In a bowl, combine wheat berries, cranberries, pecans, celery, and feta.
2. Whisk olive oil, vinegar, salt, and pepper.
3. Toss salad with dressing and serve.

Oatmeal Maple Cookies

Ingredients:

- 1 cup rolled oats
- 1 cup all-purpose flour
- 1/2 cup butter, softened
- 1/2 cup maple syrup
- 1/2 tsp cinnamon
- 1/2 tsp baking soda
- 1/4 tsp salt
- 1 egg

Instructions:

1. Preheat oven to 350°F (175°C).
2. In a bowl, mix oats, flour, cinnamon, baking soda, and salt.
3. In another bowl, cream butter and maple syrup. Beat in egg.
4. Combine wet and dry ingredients.
5. Drop spoonfuls onto a baking sheet and bake for 10-12 minutes.

Maple Butter Glazed Chicken

Ingredients:

- 4 bone-in chicken thighs
- 1/4 cup maple syrup
- 2 tbsp melted butter
- 1 tbsp Dijon mustard
- 1/2 tsp garlic powder
- 1/2 tsp salt
- 1/4 tsp black pepper

Instructions:

1. Preheat oven to 375°F (190°C).
2. Mix maple syrup, butter, mustard, garlic powder, salt, and pepper.
3. Place chicken in a baking dish and brush with glaze.
4. Bake for 35-40 minutes, basting occasionally.
5. Serve warm.

Homemade Rhubarb Crisp

Ingredients:

Filling:

- 4 cups rhubarb, chopped
- 1/2 cup sugar
- 1 tbsp cornstarch
- 1 tsp vanilla extract

Topping:

- 1 cup rolled oats
- 1/2 cup all-purpose flour
- 1/3 cup brown sugar
- 1/2 tsp cinnamon
- 1/2 cup butter, melted

Instructions:

1. Preheat oven to 375°F (190°C).
2. Toss rhubarb with sugar, cornstarch, and vanilla. Spread in a baking dish.
3. Mix oats, flour, brown sugar, cinnamon, and melted butter. Sprinkle over rhubarb.
4. Bake for 35-40 minutes until golden and bubbly. Serve warm.

Barbecue Bison Ribs

Ingredients:

- 2 lbs bison ribs
- 1 cup barbecue sauce
- 1/4 cup apple cider vinegar
- 2 cloves garlic, minced
- 1 tbsp smoked paprika
- 1 tsp salt
- 1/2 tsp black pepper

Instructions:

1. Preheat oven to 300°F (150°C).
2. Season ribs with paprika, salt, and pepper.
3. Wrap in foil and bake for 2.5-3 hours until tender.
4. In a saucepan, mix barbecue sauce, vinegar, and garlic. Simmer for 10 minutes.
5. Brush ribs with sauce and grill over medium heat for 5 minutes per side.
6. Serve with extra sauce.

Farmer's Market Vegetable Stir-Fry

Ingredients:

- 1 small zucchini, sliced
- 1 red bell pepper, sliced
- 1 cup snap peas
- 1 small carrot, julienned
- 2 cloves garlic, minced
- 1 tbsp soy sauce
- 1 tbsp sesame oil
- 1/2 tsp ginger, grated
- 1 tbsp sesame seeds

Instructions:

1. Heat sesame oil in a pan over medium-high heat.
2. Add garlic and ginger, sauté for 30 seconds.
3. Stir in vegetables and cook for 4-5 minutes until tender-crisp.
4. Add soy sauce and toss to coat.
5. Sprinkle with sesame seeds before serving.

Traditional Tourtière with Ketchup Chutney

Ingredients:

Tourtière:

- 1 lb ground pork
- 1/2 lb ground beef
- 1 small onion, finely chopped
- 2 cloves garlic, minced
- 1/2 tsp ground cinnamon
- 1/4 tsp ground cloves
- 1/2 tsp dried thyme
- 1/2 tsp salt
- 1/4 tsp black pepper
- 1/2 cup beef broth
- 1/2 cup mashed potatoes
- 1 double-crust pie dough

Ketchup Chutney:

- 1/2 cup ketchup
- 1/4 cup apple cider vinegar
- 1 tbsp brown sugar
- 1/2 tsp mustard powder
- 1/4 tsp cinnamon

Instructions:

1. Preheat oven to 375°F (190°C).
2. Cook pork and beef in a pan over medium heat until browned. Drain fat.
3. Add onion, garlic, cinnamon, cloves, thyme, salt, and pepper. Cook until onions soften.
4. Stir in broth and mashed potatoes. Let cool.
5. Roll out pie dough and place in a pie dish. Fill with meat mixture, cover with the second crust, and seal edges.
6. Bake for 35-40 minutes until golden. Cool before serving.
7. For chutney, mix all ingredients in a saucepan and simmer for 10 minutes. Serve alongside tourtière.

Smoked Trout with Horseradish Cream

Ingredients:

- 2 smoked trout fillets
- 1/2 cup sour cream
- 1 tbsp prepared horseradish
- 1 tbsp lemon juice
- 1 tbsp chopped dill
- Salt and pepper to taste

Instructions:

1. In a bowl, mix sour cream, horseradish, lemon juice, dill, salt, and pepper.
2. Serve smoked trout with horseradish cream on the side.

Apple and Cheddar Hand Pies

Ingredients:

Pastry:

- 2 cups all-purpose flour
- 1/2 tsp salt
- 1/2 cup cold butter, cubed
- 1/4 cup cold water

Filling:

- 2 apples, peeled and diced
- 1/2 cup shredded cheddar cheese
- 2 tbsp brown sugar
- 1/2 tsp cinnamon
- 1 egg, beaten (for egg wash)

Instructions:

1. Preheat oven to 375°F (190°C).
2. Mix flour and salt. Cut in butter until crumbly. Add water and mix until dough forms. Chill for 30 minutes.
3. In a bowl, toss apples with cheddar, sugar, and cinnamon.
4. Roll out dough and cut into circles. Place filling on one half, fold over, and crimp edges.
5. Brush with egg wash and bake for 20-25 minutes until golden.

Wild Rice and Lentil Pilaf

Ingredients:

- 1/2 cup wild rice
- 1/2 cup lentils, rinsed
- 3 cups vegetable broth
- 1 small onion, diced
- 2 cloves garlic, minced
- 1/2 tsp dried thyme
- 1 tbsp olive oil
- Salt and pepper to taste

Instructions:

1. In a pot, heat olive oil and sauté onion and garlic until soft.
2. Add wild rice, lentils, thyme, salt, and pepper. Stir for 1 minute.
3. Pour in broth, bring to a boil, reduce heat, and simmer for 40-45 minutes until rice and lentils are tender.
4. Fluff with a fork and serve warm.

Cranberry Scones

Ingredients:

- 2 cups all-purpose flour
- 1/4 cup sugar
- 1 tbsp baking powder
- 1/2 tsp salt
- 1/2 cup cold butter, cubed
- 1/2 cup dried cranberries
- 3/4 cup milk
- 1 tsp vanilla extract

Instructions:

1. Preheat oven to 375°F (190°C).
2. Mix flour, sugar, baking powder, and salt in a bowl.
3. Cut in butter until mixture is crumbly. Stir in cranberries.
4. Add milk and vanilla. Mix until dough forms.
5. Shape into a disc, cut into wedges, and bake for 18-20 minutes.

Maple-Glazed Roast Chicken

Ingredients:

- 1 whole chicken (4-5 lbs)
- 1/4 cup maple syrup
- 2 tbsp Dijon mustard
- 2 tbsp melted butter
- 2 cloves garlic, minced
- 1 tsp dried thyme
- 1/2 tsp black pepper
- 1 tbsp apple cider vinegar

Instructions:

1. Preheat oven to 375°F (190°C).
2. Mix maple syrup, mustard, butter, garlic, thyme, pepper, and vinegar.
3. Pat chicken dry and place in a roasting pan. Brush with glaze.
4. Roast for 1 hour 15 minutes, basting every 20 minutes.
5. Let rest for 10 minutes before carving.

Venison Chili

Ingredients:

- 1 lb ground venison
- 1 small onion, chopped
- 1 red bell pepper, chopped
- 2 cloves garlic, minced
- 1 can (14 oz) diced tomatoes
- 1 can (15 oz) kidney beans, drained
- 1 cup beef broth
- 1 tbsp chili powder
- 1/2 tsp cumin
- 1/2 tsp smoked paprika
- Salt and pepper to taste

Instructions:

1. In a pot, cook venison over medium heat until browned. Drain excess fat.
2. Add onion, bell pepper, and garlic. Cook until softened.
3. Stir in tomatoes, kidney beans, broth, and spices.
4. Simmer for 30 minutes. Adjust seasoning and serve warm.

Roasted Chestnut and Mushroom Soup

Ingredients:

- 1 cup roasted chestnuts, chopped
- 1 cup mushrooms, sliced
- 1 small onion, chopped
- 2 cloves garlic, minced
- 3 cups vegetable broth
- 1/2 cup heavy cream
- 1 tbsp olive oil
- 1/2 tsp thyme
- Salt and pepper to taste

Instructions:

1. In a pot, heat olive oil and sauté onion, garlic, and mushrooms until soft.
2. Add chestnuts, broth, thyme, salt, and pepper. Simmer for 15 minutes.
3. Blend until smooth, then stir in heavy cream. Serve warm.

Rye Bread with Flax Seeds

Ingredients:

- 2 cups rye flour
- 1 cup all-purpose flour
- 1/4 cup ground flax seeds
- 1 packet (2 1/4 tsp) active dry yeast
- 1 tsp salt
- 1 cup warm water
- 1 tbsp honey
- 1 tbsp olive oil

Instructions:

1. Dissolve yeast in warm water with honey. Let sit for 5 minutes.
2. In a bowl, mix flours, flax seeds, and salt. Add yeast mixture and olive oil.
3. Knead for 8-10 minutes until smooth. Cover and let rise for 1 hour.
4. Shape into a loaf, place in a greased pan, and let rise for another 30 minutes.
5. Preheat oven to 375°F (190°C) and bake for 30-35 minutes. Cool before slicing.

Pumpkin Seed and Cranberry Energy Bites

Ingredients:

- 1 cup rolled oats
- 1/2 cup pumpkin seeds
- 1/4 cup dried cranberries
- 1/4 cup honey
- 1/4 cup almond butter
- 1/2 tsp cinnamon

Instructions:

1. In a bowl, mix oats, pumpkin seeds, cranberries, cinnamon, honey, and almond butter.
2. Roll into small balls and refrigerate for 30 minutes before serving.

Maple-Glazed Donuts

Ingredients:

Doughnuts:

- 2 cups all-purpose flour
- 1/4 cup sugar
- 1 tbsp baking powder
- 1/2 tsp salt
- 1/2 cup milk
- 1 egg
- 3 tbsp butter, melted
- 1 tsp vanilla extract
- Oil for frying

Glaze:

- 1/2 cup pure maple syrup
- 1 cup powdered sugar
- 1 tbsp milk

Instructions:

1. Mix flour, sugar, baking powder, and salt in a bowl.
2. In another bowl, whisk milk, egg, butter, and vanilla. Combine with dry ingredients.
3. Roll out dough and cut into doughnut shapes.
4. Heat oil in a fryer to 350°F (175°C) and fry doughnuts for 1-2 minutes per side.
5. For glaze, whisk maple syrup, powdered sugar, and milk.
6. Dip warm doughnuts in glaze and let set before serving.